HUGH JOHNSON'S
Cellar Book

Owing to the recent bombardment,
it is preferable for the Red Wine to be decanted.

Wine List at Prunier's Restaurant, London May 1941

HUGH JOHNSON'S

Cellar Book

MITCHELL BEAZLEY

Hugh Johnson's Cellar Book

First published in Great Britain in 1986 as *The Hugh Johnson Cellar Book* by Mitchell Beazley, an imprint of Reed Consumer Books Limited, Michelin House, 81 Fulham Road, London, SW3 6RB

Revised editions 1993, 1998

ISBN 1 84000 093 7

A CIP catalogue record for this book is available from the British Library

Commissioning Editor: Sue Jamieson
Executive Art Editor: Fiona Knowles
Editor: Hilary Lumsden
Illustrations: Jill Raphaeline
Production Controller: Rachel Lynch

Typeset in ITC Novarese and New Caledonia

Printed and bound by Toppan Printing Company, China

Contents

Introduction

The traditional cellar record book was conceived in an age when the range of wines was definitely finite: perhaps only 20 or 30 wines if you were lucky. Its object was simply to keep track of the number of bottles consumed. I have what appears to be the first cellar book on my desk. It was published in the 1750s by R & J Dodsley in Pall Mall, London. Beside the spaces for the tally of bottles is a single narrow column headed "memorandum". Two specimen memoranda are given: "Claret from Mr ..." and "Lord ... dined here". Either, I thought, could make a rather neat title for this cellar book. For it is more about the memorandum than the tally.

The record-keeping problem today is not the number of bottles: it is the number of wines. A keen amateur may buy several dozen of any single one. A tally is still important; bottles can easily be mislaid in crowded racks. But even more vital is the note that reminds you of the taste of the wine, its quality, its value and the food and the friends that went with it.

The layout of this cellar book, therefore, allots considerably more space to smaller quantities of wine, or even individual bottles, than it does to more sizeable parcels of wine – comprising large numbers of cases – that make their stately way through perhaps two decades of your life.

Fine red Bordeaux bought *en primeur*, at its first appearance on the market, is delivered to you between two and three years old. If you have bought a dozen you may taste the first bottle straight away to make its acquaintance, but the next bottle not for five years, and the next (if it is really good wine) not for another five. Then, when you are convinced it has reached the potential you paid for, you drink all but two bottles – which you probably keep out of nostalgia, or in case you should miss still further improvement. Eventually its page of biography makes wonderful nostalgic reading – not perhaps so useful, though, as the precise name of a miraculous Italian estate wine which you found on holiday, brought home, enjoyed, entered in the book and fully intend buying again, as soon as you can find it.

Both wines have their place. Both also have their context. Where a meal has been made memorable by a particularly happy matching of several wines with appropriate dishes in appropriate company, the entire occasion deserves to be noted down. Space is provided for such memorable meals, which can be cross-referred to the wine pages.

Whether you make wine your earnest study, a diverting pastime, or simply want to know, as it were, where you have been, a record of the comings and goings of your cellar is well worth keeping. The same is true whether your "cellar" is a vaulted chamber, a space under the stairs or simply the combined resources of the wine merchants you frequent.

Why a wine cellar?

The pleasure of possession is nothing to be ashamed of. To have a good picture on the wall, a good car in the garage, a splendid tree shading your house, a beautiful watch on your wrist are all matters for legitimate satisfaction. And so is a cellar of good wine. To know that in your cupboard (or even better, beneath your feet) you have well-chosen wine maturing is a grand comfort to anyone's life. Nor is it a purely selfish pleasure. Wine is, after all, the most sociable collectable. Buying wine to keep and mature is a hostly and generous habit. The time, the trouble, the space it takes are all in the worthy service of hospitality. When the wine is ripe and ready you will share it with your friends. The purpose of fine wine is much more than mere

refreshment: it is to awaken faculties that demand expression, to bring minds together in sharing a common pleasure.

The pleasure is all the greater when the wine is in perfect condition, well-chosen, well-stored, well-matured and well-served. Greater still when you, having played the role of guardian, find your charge surpasses its early promise.

This is the true purpose of keeping your own wine cellar, however modest or magnificent. It is the only way you can be sure of a supply of the wine you want when it is at its best. There are other rewards for the pains that you take: you will save money, and may find you have made a crafty investment. You will never again find yourself panting home with an armful of bottles that you suspect have been dumped and are certainly all shaken up and at the wrong temperature for dinner. You can buy when you have the money, claim discounts for quantity, have the wine delivered at leisure. You will certainly spend therapeutic hours handling bottles, re-reading labels, speculating on flavours. Better still, when you drink the wine, it feels like a gift from a fairy godmother. Money spent years ago is money gone. Wine you eventually drink is free – or so it feels.

How to use this book

A cellar book is distinct from a wine-taster's note book rather in the way that a visitors' book differs from a diary. Many enthusiastic wine-lovers keep jotting-pads for their impressions of every wine that comes their way. Such notes are essential to wine professionals. They are also one of the quickest aids to learning wine for amateurs. A cellar book serves some of the same purposes, but its prime point is the recording and management of the wines of a single household: to plot their purchase, storage and consumption so that nothing is wasted or forgotten, every bottle is given its full value at its due time and the proceedings put on record for reference or recollection.

The procedure is the same whatever the size of the cellar. (The word "cellar", be it noted, means "stock of wine"; any poetic connotations suggesting vaults, arches, pillars, flagged floors, creaking doors, jangling chains and long perspectives of stacked bottles glimpsed by lantern-light are incidental. Highly enjoyable too.)

All acquisitions of wine are classed as either "current" or "for stock". Current wines are not normally entered in detail on a full page. But it is useful and interesting (and can be impressive) to note the number of bottles that pass through the household for instant consumption. Space is reserved at the end of the book for this simple tally function. Note that wines entered here should be used (or almost) before more are entered.

Wines acquired "for stock" should be entered with full details of their origins and provenance, in either of the *Cellar notes* sections, depending on the quantity. Your habits will dictate whether six, one dozen or three dozen bottles is a major purchase demanding two pages of its own. Bear in mind the longevity factor as well as the number of bottles. Six long-term bottles of high quality may merit a full entry where half a dozen

one- to two-year-old bottles are more appropriately allotted a two- or four-line space in the second of the *Cellar notes* sections.

The time to enter all wines is immediately on purchase, when all details are fresh in your memory. In some cases there may be no space in racks and the wine will remain in its box as delivered. In some cases there may be no space at all and the wine is stored at the supplying merchants. Enter it nonetheless as part of your stock and make a pencil note of where the wine is until you are able to unpack it and allot it a "permanent" position in your racks.

In the case of wines bought *en primeur* (which is to say while they are still in their makers' cellars) you get nothing for your money, except a receipt, for up to three years. In addition to filing these important receipts in a safe place it is a good idea to note *en primeur* orders, perhaps in their destined positions in either of the *Cellar notes* sections.

A coding system for locating bottles in stock without wasting space in your racks is suggested on page 18. Enter the codes into the *Location in the cellar* section of the appropriate page, at the time you allocate spaces to the bottles. Delete the codes as you drink the bottles. You thus have a perfect, up-to-date record of the number and location of each and every bottle of your wine.

The time to fill in each of the other columns is there and then (or here and now). Delay even a day and some interesting detail will escape you. Your notes on the wines may range from "great" to a short essay, but they should be immediate. Your summary of the occasion, food and company is best done at the same time. This will provide the most precise and effective reference.

The *Memorable meals* section offers scope for the recording of notable occasions, dinner or lunch parties, in album fashion. Its plan is flexible enough to accommodate either a simple record

Wine details

Name **Ch. Langoa-Barton**

Vintage **1980**

Grower/Bottler/Shipper **CB**

Where acquired **Wine Club**

Quantity **12**

Bottle size **Bott's**

Price **£71**

Date ordered **June '81**

Date received **Sept '82**

Location in cellar

B6	D6	E1	H1	J3
B7	D7	E2	H2	I4
B8	D8	E3	H3	J5
B9	D9	E4	H9	J6

Repeat orders

Critics' comments

'One of the v. delicious wines of the vintage' R.P.

Serving record

Date	Occasion	Bottles used	Bottles remaining
1 Dec '82	Tasting with other '80's S.R., R.A.C., Judy, J.T.T.	1	11
3 Mar '83	Supper with Judy (couldn't wait!)	1	10
10 Jul '83	Summer evening in the garden, Ghristhisse, Duncan, Carole	4	6
21 May '84	Dinner after Chelsea B&D, C&J	1	5

Country/Region: **Bordeaux**

Food/Other Wines	Comments	Tally
Branaire-Ducru, G-Larose, Leoville-L, Beychevelle	Still oaky, but gently rich and forward. Stood out in group as v. well made.	B6 B8 B9
Grilled chicken, German blue brie	Remarkably smooth and easy already, but not lacking guts. Spicy in the middle. Keep trying!	D9 E2 E4
Barbecue. Pol Roger NV artichokes, steaks, cheddar	Why isn't more Claret like this? Served quite cool from cellar, brilliantly refreshing - satisfying at the same time. Mustn't finish it.	H1 H2 H9 I4 I5 I6
Chignot '73, C-Charlemagne '78 L-B '66 Cold salmon, leg of lamb (veg, new pots)	Admirable intro to the '66, but it will never reach its stature.	

30

31

or something more evocative. A good visitors' book contains tributes, sketches and snapshots – and of course signatures. Memorable meals may deserve a page of all these, plus a label from a bottle that gave great pleasure.

Use this book, therefore, with enough method and discipline to make it a useful – in fact essential – tool. But also use it to paint a portrait of yourself, your friends and your enjoyment in wine.

Above: The double page spreads in the first Cellar notes section provide ample space for a complete biography of wine. Its vital statistics are filled in on delivery, then tasting notes build up the picture as the consignment is slowly consumed. The Location in the cellar section (bottom left) allows a quick check on stock levels.

Planning your cellar: what to buy

Family, friends, age, taste, habits, income, accommodation, expectations, degree of interest in wine, availability of good wines – all these are among the variables that mean no two cellars are, can be or should be the same. There is no such thing as an ideal cellar for all purposes or all people. The only theoretically ideal cellar it would be possible to collect would be one with the sole purpose of investment. It would be a predictable collection of blue-chip names, almost all Bordeaux and vintage port; in other words anything but ideal for experiment, entertainment, exploration or simple enjoyment.

Your cellar should follow no norms or predictable patterns; it should reflect your own preferences and the pace of your life. Wines are increasingly subject to the whims of fashion as more and more wine journalists echo each other round the world. A fashionable cellar is almost certainly bad value for money. By all means follow up the recommendations of books, articles and newsletters. But do not be led by the nose. Be sceptical about convenient scoring systems that rate all wines with points out of ten, 20 or even, more extravagantly, 100. The notion that there is such a thing as an 86/100 wine, consistently better than an 85/100 wine, is transparent folly.

"I very rarely bought more at a time than a single dozen of each wine named, nay, half a dozen or even odd bottles by way of experiment. In wine, as in books and other things, I have tried to be a (very minor) Ulysses, steering ever from the known to the unknown."

George Saintsbury. Notes on a Cellar-book, 1920.

Taste highly-recommended and fashionable wines, but ask yourself the cold question: do they give you greater pleasure corresponding to a higher price?

As with all goods that you buy regularly, but are subject to variation, it is better to establish a friendly and confident relationship with one or more suppliers, who will appreciate your custom and do their best to deserve your trust, than to try to outsmart the market.

"It should be carefully remembered that no bottle of old wine, of a given growth, is identical with another of the same growth and of the same vintage. Not only are there bad, indifferent, average and good bottles, but, among the best, each has its own particular character. If you open ten bottles of 1870 Cos d'Estournel you will get different wines."

Paul de Cassagnac. French Wines.
Translated by Guy Knowles, 1936.

Let your cellar develop its own character. Don't try to be all-knowing, but follow, vintage by vintage, particular wines that you have enjoyed. There is much pleasure in specialising. The small differences between two neighbouring châteaux in one specific area, over a series of vintages, will soon become significant once you get to know them well. Consequently they will probably give you as much pleasure as some more obvious (and expensive) contrasts. If you are lucky enough to know a wine-producer personally why not buy, enjoy and talk about his wine? Make it, as it were, your own.

The most impressive and unusual private cellar I ever saw was situated under a dignified stone-built 18th-century rectory in the west of England. It was approached by either of two stately flights of stone steps, shallow in the tread and broad enough for two to walk abreast. They descended into a broad, squarish, stone-flagged chamber, lit by three or four embrasures only, and cloistered all round with the comforting arches of bottle-bins, arch over arch like the Pont du Gard. The Rector, you might imagine, entered from the right, and while conversing, chose the bottles to be brought up by his butler. Making his exit to the left, he then remarked to his companion how agreeably cool the wine would be.

Stately as it all was, what really fixed it in my mind forever was the evidence of the last incumbent's taste, the names were chalked on the slates that hung one above each empty bin. There was no heterodoxy about this parson. Bollinger, the labels read, Veuve Clicquot-Ponsardin, Moët et Chandon, Krug. Below them Laurent Perrier, Heidsieck, Ayala, Pommery. On the right were Pol Roger, Mumm, Taittinger. To the left sat Lanson, Perrier Jouët, Irroy, Goulet, Roederer, Mercier, Piper, Gratien, Gosset, Ruinart and Jacquesson.

I have often pondered upon this parson. Fond of Champagne, I wouldn't wonder. The only question that bothers me is how on earth did he make up his mind?

As one who like as not goes to the cupboard for a bottle of sherry and, three-quarters of an hour later, comes out with two half-bottles of claret, I admire him prodigiously. "Gosset", do you think he exclaimed on waking, "it's a Gosset day"? Or was he indecisive, torn between the multiple alternatives, constantly distracted in his sermon-writing by the need to decide between Moët et Chandon and Mumm before luncheon?

Remember that wine is for people, it gives pleasure in many ways beside the relatively rarefied one of taste. Indulge in and buy the wines of your children's and your friends' children's birth years, or of any year that may be of special significance for you. Children are proud of "their" wine, and when you open a bottle from the year of your wedding it is not the bouquet, the residual sugar or the after-taste that is uppermost in your mind.

"One should also note that some wine dealers cheat people when they taste their wines. They make bitter and sour wines appear sweet by persuading the wine-tasters to eat first licorice or nuts or old salty cheese or dishes that have been well-cooked with spices ... The wine-tasters can protect themselves against such doings by tasting wine in the morning after they have rinsed their mouths and eaten three or four bites of bread dipped in water, for whoever tries out a wine on a quite empty or on a quite full stomach will find his mouth and his tasting spoiled."

Arnaldus de Villanova. Liber de Vinis.
From the German of Wilhelm von Himkofen, 1478.

When you find a splendid wine that will keep and improve for years, link it to a particular day of the year or occasion. We have a store of rich Oloroso sherry that has become The Christmas Wine. One bottle is opened each year on Christmas morning. Each Christmas it is even better. The wine is maturing beautifully, but even more important is the cargo of happy associations it carries through the years.

Wine classification

It is helpful, although artificial, to categorise all the wines you buy into age-brackets. Drinking age, that is. The better the wine, the less certainty there is about its ultimate optimum age, but it is practical and not unrealistic to use the categories below to classify your purchases.

Drink-up wines

To be drunk from hand to mouth. Do not buy more than you will use within three months.

The great majority of low-price red and white wines. "Jug wines". Reds and whites sold as Nouveau, Beaujolais style. Most brand-name table wines. Most Italian white wines. Muscadet. The rare Condrieu. Vinho Verde. Fino sherry. German wines below the Qualitätswein level. Most "blush", rosé or *oeil de perdrix* wines and *vins gris*. Plain Côtes-du-Rhône and Chianti.

All wines in this class rely on their freshness for their appeal and can only lose it by being kept.

One–two year wines

A large category of both red and white wine whose character and value increase quite rapidly in the years immediately after bottling. Too fresh, these wines can be either "dumb", hiding their full flavours, or "harsh", distracting you from them.

Examples among white wines are Chablis, Sancerre, regular-quality Alsace, German Qualitätswein, most Chenin Blanc, good Swiss wines, regular-quality Chardonnays (whether from Burgundy, California, Australia, New Zealand, Chile or any other source). Among reds, Bordeaux and Bourgogne Rouge, Côtes-du-Rhône-Villages and the better Midi and Provence reds, Reserva wines from Italy and Spain, almost all moderate-priced Cabernet Sauvignon reds. Most wines, in fact, in which you hope to find vigour, some body, pronounced character, but not the complex and ethereal bouquet that comes with long evolution.

Champagne, both vintage and non-vintage, should be included in this category, at least in Europe. Further afield non-vintage Champagne has often matured sufficiently (and occasionally too much) *en route*. Late-bottled vintage and "crusting" ports can benefit from one or two years' cellaring. So can high-quality Oloroso sherries.

"There is no money, among that which I have spent since I began to earn my living, of the expenditure of which I am less ashamed, or which gave me better value in return, than the price of the liquids chronicled in this booklet."

George Saintsbury. Notes on a Cellar-book, 1920.

Two–five year wines

It is a question of degree which wines fall into this, the previous and the next categories. Degree, above all, of quality. The best examples of wines in this class often only begin gaining in flavour and interest after two years or more in the bottle, putting on real style towards and sometimes considerably beyond their fifth years.

Examples are *crus bourgeois* Bordeaux and their equivalents from other regions in good vintages – for instance 1989 Médocs in 1997; 1994s in 1998 and the majority of Côte d'Or red burgundies (Beaune, Volnay, Savigny, Chambolle and so on) in normal vintages – 1987, 1989 and 1992 were all at their best at about five years. Five years is a good age for high-quality wines from such light vintages as Bordeaux 1991 and for Cahors, Madiran and the mid-weight reds. More concentrated wines – top California and Australian reds as well as great Bordeaux vintages – are prone to go into a chrysalis at this stage, tasting thick and disappointing, as though a veil needs to lift to reveal their qualities. But for most quality reds from Italy, Spain and the New World these days, five years is a good age.

All the best white burgundies and other Chardonnays belong in this category, along with the majority of high-quality Rhône, Alsace and Bordeaux whites. German and Austrian Kabinett and some Spätlese and Auslese. Many Sauternes (but not the best) begin to taste good at this stage. Few other wines should be kept much longer, with some exotic exceptions (for example, Hunter Valley Semillon, Jurançon and the very rare top-quality dry white Bordeaux). Great vintage Champagnes belong in this class, unless you appreciate the deeper flavours of age – the hint of Madeira, known to the French as, *"le goût anglais"*.

Long-term whites

Only exceptional white wines call for maturing beyond five years, but a few demand it. They are the highest qualities of white burgundy in vintages of exceptional balance, their equivalents from Germany: perfect Spätlese and Auslese almost always from the Riesling grape. The world's greatest sweet wines, the best Sauternes and Barsacs, German Beerenauslese, Trockenbeerenauslese and Eiswein. And since the rebirth of Tokay in 1991 the greater Aszú vintages of this apparently immortal wine.

"It is an error to suppose the wine which will keep long should only be drank when it will keep no longer."

Cyrus Redding.
A History and Description of Modern Wines, 1833.

Long-term reds

The world's finest red wines all come into this category. Their high natural tannin content usually needs a minimum of ten and often up to 20 years' ageing to combine with the pigments in the still-mysterious and fascinating process of bottle maturation.

Good quality classed-growth Bordeaux of successful vintages are the slowest of natural wines to resolve themselves. But very good red burgundies have almost as much to gain by ten years or more years in the bottle. Other wines that evolve from burly to beautiful over a similar period of time are the best Rhône reds –

above all Hermitage; Barolo and Barbaresco from Piedmont, Brunello and Sassicaia from Tuscany; certain rare Rioja Gran Reservas and Vega Sicilia (Ribera del Duero) from Spain.

The best Cabernet Sauvignons of California, plus a few exceptional Australian reds, also have this wonderful capacity to age, although the great majority (even of the finest quality) are made to drink in the first ten years of their life – a conscious decision on the part of the consumer.

The longest-term wine of all for ageing is vintage port. Few vintage ports and certainly no great ones begin to be exciting or manage to give the ultimate pleasure to their consumer before they have slept for at least 15 years in the bottle. Almost certainly, great vintages (1977 is a good example) are still young at 25 years or so.

"The young Prince had forborn wine all the last year, by reason of an inflammation in his Throat occasion'd by his hard drinking; with which his Father also had been formerly troubl'd for the same cause. Which was the reason that the Kourouk, or prohibition of wine was renew'd, to the end there might be no more sold. For it is the custom of the Grandees in Asia, when they have an intention to abandon wine, they send orders to throw away all that they have, and to knock out the heads of the vessels, to the end that if they should have a desire to drink again, they might not have an opportunity to satisfie themselves; not looking upon themselves to be Masters of their Passions."

Sir John Chardin. Travels into Persia, 1686.

Buy more of slower wine

In deciding how much of any one wine to buy, price is naturally the first consideration. But do not forget the longevity factor: the longer a wine can be expected to continue maturing, the more you will eventually need (or wish you had). If you buy six bottles of a ten-year wine you may open one when you buy it, another three years later to observe progress, another after five or six years, another (impatiently) at eight. Ten years arrives, the wine is becoming glorious, but you only have two bottles left. If you had bought a dozen there would be enough for two or three dinner parties. With two dozen you would have the opportunity of selling a complete case at a wine auction to finance re-stocking, with full knowledge of the qualities of what you were selling.

Taking a collection of wines as a whole, the formula for the ideal number of bottles is:

annual consumption x optimum ageing time = ideal stock

So if a given type of wine needs to be kept for, on average, five years and consumption is two bottles a month, the ideal stock is: 24(annual consumption) x five(average ageing time) = 120 bottles.

The replacement figure – the number of bottles which must be bought each year – is the same as the annual consumption. The costs are expressed in pounds sterling, but the formula works just as well in dollars – just multiply by the prevailing exchange rate. Prices for the various types of wines will of course vary from country to country.

	Type	Consumption	Ideal stock	Replacement rate/year	Cost
WHITE WINE	Drink-up whites	Max. stock 12 bottles			
	1–2 year whites at £60	1 bottle/week	52 x 1.5 =78	52	x £5 = £260
	Long-term whites (3–10 years) at £120	2 bottles/month	24 x 6.5 =156	24	x £10 – £240
			Total = 234 bottles = 19½ cases		Total = £500/year
RED WINE	Drink-up reds	Max. stock 12 bottles			
	1–2 year reds at £48	2 bottles/week	104 x 1.5 =156	104	x £4 = £416
	2–5 year reds at £78	1 bottle/week	52 x 3.5 = 182	52	x £6 = £312
	Long-term reds (5–20 years) at £180	Average 1 bottle/month	12 x 20 = 120	12	x £15 = £180
			Total = 458 bottles = 38 cases		Total = £908/year
			Grand total = 57 cases		**Grand total = £1408/year**

Storage conditions

Security, darkness, temperature and humidity are the four factors to consider. Wine storage should be dark. Light, particularly its ultra-violet component, penetrates even dark green bottle glass surprisingly easily and with quickly damaging effects. A bottle of wine exposed in a window or under the lights of a store for a mere few weeks will suffer chemical changes. Do not buy such a bottle – and do not keep bottles in such places at home.

Wine should be stored at a constant temperature. Whether as low as 40°F (5°C) or as high as 70°F (21°C) is probably not important in the short or medium term, although the lower the temperature the slower the rate of biochemical change – be it for improvement or deterioration. The two enemies of wine are excessively high temperature, certainly anything above about 70°F, and rapid or extreme fluctuations repeated over a significant period of time. Such fluctuations expand and contract the wine in the bottle and can make the cork "weep". Probably more important they simply "tire" the wine and sap its organic vitality. Wines that have been shifted from one cellar to another several times in their lives are less likely to reach full maturity with all their qualities intact. Witness the fact that an auction catalogue will always note if a wine has lain all its life in one cellar – and stress, very often, that the cellar was a cold one, where development would be as slow and steady as possible.

There is, surprisingly, little evidence that cold, even freezing temperatures will harm a wine, at least over a short period. Bottles have occasionally been frozen solid and gently thawed without detectable change, the greatest risk being that expansion will force the cork out. Months of deep chill however seems to have the effect of numbing the flavour so that it may never recover.

Extreme heat on the contrary is rapidly fatal. A distressing amount of the wine landed in summer in hot climates (including the Eastern United States) spends long enough in primitive dockside storage, or in a container exposed to the sun, to age it prematurely. To survive the tropics all natural-strength wines need temperature-controlled transit and storage.

"I have met with persons in England who imagine the sobriety of a French table carried to such a length, that one or two glasses of wine are all that a man can get at dinner; this is an error; your servant mixes the wine and water in what proportion you please; and large bowls of clean glasses are set ... at different posts of the table, for serving the richer and rarer sorts of wines, which are drunk in this manner freely enough. The whole nation are splendidly neat in refusing to drink out of glasses used by other people."

Arthur Young. Travels in France
during the years 1787, 1788 and 1789.

In practical terms for a householder the most important factor is insulation. Cellars are dug in the ground for the sake of its insulation. There is still no better way. At best the insulation provided by thick walls, or double walls filled with foam, can be very effective in slowing the rate of heating or cooling – effective enough in the temperate climate of northwestern Europe. Wine in cases maintains a more level temperature than bottles in racks.

In more extreme climates the heat loss or gain each time the door is opened soon means that a heating and/or cooling unit is needed. The whole cellar can be air-conditioned, or a chilled cabinet used to store the white wines. Air-conditioning should be set at about 50°F (10°C) to achieve both the ideal storage temperature for all wines and a close-to-ideal temperature for serving most white wines and Champagne.

Humidity is the friend of wine but the enemy of labels and cartons. A cellar can scarcely be too damp for a bare bottle. In a dry cellar the cork must rely on the wine at one end to keep it moist and tight-fitting. In a damp one the whole cork is evenly saturated. The evidence of certain very wet cellars is that wines age more slowly under these conditions. Their labels, however, age instantly, become unreadable and fall off. Unless your cellar records are perfect you may lose the identity of the wine. A bottle cannot be resold at auction or otherwise without a label – in that flimsy piece of paper lies all its tradeable value...

A coat of varnish, or a squirt of hair-lacquer, is a vey useful protective measure against the sort of moderate damp that will cause mildew to form on labels over a period of years. But a dripping crypt is not a place to collect wine.

....

"Burgundy of the first class will support itself to twenty years, but after twelve or fourteen it does not in the least improve; and the third year in bottle, or the sixth from the vintage, is the time when it is most perfect in every good quality. Good Champagne, on the contrary, will often be found to improve for ten or fifteen years, and will support itself until thirty, and sometimes until it is forty years old... On the other hand, hock is not in full perfection until it is forty years old, and it will keep well four times that term."

Cyrus Redding. A History and Description of Modern Wines. 1833.

....

Store all wine prone so that the liquid is in contact with the cork. The cork in a standing bottle, especially in a dry atmosphere, will lose its spongy resilience quite rapidly, in say a month or two, allowing air to reach the wine. On one, apparently unique, occasion the cork in a standing bottle shrank enough to fall into the wine and yet the lead capsule, with the thin film of fungus that had formed inside it, maintained an airtight seal. The fact was discovered ten years later – and the wine was still sound.

There are two arcane exceptions to the lying-down rule: Tokay and Barolo. The sweetest Tokays were traditionally stored standing in damp cellars and recorked every ten years or so. Some traditional Barolo-makers follow the same practice; but more, it seems, from ignorance than secret knowledge.

Much can be seen of the character and condition of wine in its bottle without pulling the cork and tasting it. While green bottle glass effectively hides the colour of white wines, those (such as Sauternes) that are bottled in clear glass declare their state of maturity instantly – a deep gold Sauternes is aged long enough; one that is turning brown should be drunk quickly.

The colour of red wine shows up well through green glass. Hold the neck of the bottle between yourself and a 60-watt light bulb. Compare the light red of an inexpensive young Bordeaux with the profound colour of a young, grand wine from a good vintage. Compare the pale purple of new Beaujolais with the fuller red of burgundy (still paler than Bordeaux), and with the translucent amber-pink of old burgundy in its bottle neck.

Good red wines from California and Australia are normally very dense in colour and remain so for longer than all except Bordeaux of exceptional vintages. Port is hard to examine, being bottled in almost black glass.

Every cellar needs permanent racks, niches, pigeonholes or bins in which the bottles are laid away. "Bins" are the relic of days when wine was bought a barrel at a time, bottled in the cellar and stacked, the whole 300-odd bottles from a barrel, usually without labels, in an arched cavity where the bottles lay two rows deep, stacked twelve layers high. They are still found in active use in châteaux and the caves of other wine-producing properties; occasionally in hotels and restaurants; but they no longer suit the purposes of private wine-collectors, whose unit is not the barrel but the bottle or case of a dozen bottles.

For our purposes the most practical form of storage is the one that takes least space. There is only one method whereby all the space can be in use all the time. The wine rack, with single-bottle openings, admittedly takes up more space itself than a format in which bottle is piled on bottle. But every bottle is accessible without moving others. As one bottle is used another can be put in its space. Its regular honeycomb pattern makes record-keeping straight forward. It is only a very busy cellar, where bottles are regularly delivered and consumed in dozen lots, that justifies the various alternative forms of racks. These accommodate several bottles in a single square or diamond-shaped opening.

Allotting spaces

It is only a very spacious cellar that can afford to have many empty places in it. Efficient storage is full storage. But as bottles are removed to be drunk empty spaces appear at random. To rearrange all the bottles continually is time-consuming – it also disturbs their beneficial repose. The only logical and efficient way to fill random spaces is as they appear, at random. Rather than trying to keep half a dozen or a dozen bottles of one wine all together, the best way to dispose of them is wherever there is room – with the essential qualification that you make a methodical note of which spaces you put them in. The *Location in cellar* space in the first *Cellar notes* section and the *Location* space in the second *Cellar notes* section of this book are designed for this purpose. Fill them in, as on the specimen page (*see* page 9), at the same time as you allot spaces to arriving bottles. In a very simple storage system of one rack there is no difficulty in giving a number to each space. Letter the horizontal ranks with "A" for the top row; number the vertical ranks with "1" for the left-hand column. Thus space "C4" is the fourth space from the left in the third row down (*see* page 19).

In a cellar with several racks each rack must be given a name or number. A spacious cellar might have separate racks for Bordeaux, Burgundy etc. A catalogue entry might then read "B'x E6", "B'y C4" or even "Left B'x" or "Top B'x E6". An alternative is to give each rack a simple number so that a catalogue entry would read "3E6".

Wine racks are normally made one bottle deep, but they can also be bought or made two bottles deep. This gives the alternative of storing two bottles both from the same side (in other words, when the wine rack is set against a wall), or when two wine racks are set back to back in a free-standing position. If bottles are stored two deep against the wall it can be difficult to see whether an opening contains one bottle or two. If there are two bottles, the front one stands proud of the rack; when only one bottle is left, push it flush with the front of the rack to indicate there is nothing behind it. Magnums in quantity present a separate storage problem. A moderate number can simply be kept on the open top of a bottle-size rack.

Name

Vintage

Grower/Bottler/Shipper

Merchant

Quantity

Bottle size

Price

Date ordered

Date received

Location in cellar

D	7									

Repeat orders

Critics comments

Above: This bottle is now No. D7 in the space logging system. When bought, it was stored in the first empty hole, and the grid number entered into the cellar book.

Bottle sizes

There is a lack of conclusive evidence to prove whether the standard wine bottle we know so well developed as a portion for one person or two. Judging by our ancestors' capacity it may well have been one man's ration. Today it is commonly considered enough for a couple.

The standard size is settling today on 75 centilitres, although inexpensive wines in certain regions are still bottled in 70 centilitre bottles. Fine wines, however, particularly Bordeaux and Champagne, are regularly bottled in a range of sizes. Their names, capacities and dimensions are listed below.

There are practical reasons for the larger sizes of bottle. In the case of Champagne they are purely celebratory – to be able to uncork 16 bottles with a single pop is a lavish gesture. In the case of Bordeaux and burgundy (although burgundy is less commonly bottled in the larger "formats") bigger bottles are theoretically essential for gatherings of eight or more, to make sure that all are drinking exactly the same wine.

As wine ages, each bottle matures in a very slightly different way. By the time fine claret is 15 years old the different characters of different bottles become quite obvious. Unless everyone at table is drinking from the same bottle they may find themselves discussing quite different wines, unable to agree; even at risk of coming to blows. At large parties where the wine is merely convivial such niceties are considered unimportant. Where

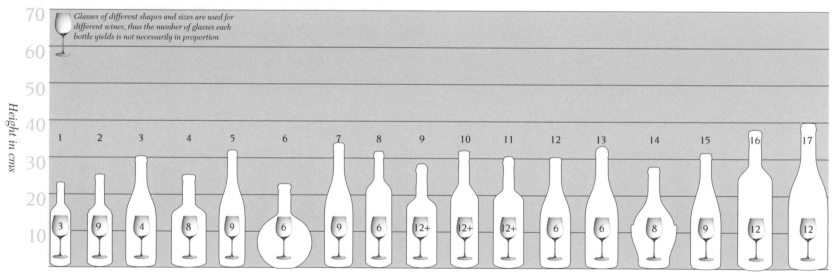

Glasses of different shapes and sizes are used for different wines, thus the number of glasses each bottle yields is not necessarily in proportion

Height in cms

KEY:
1. *Half bottle: 0.375 litre, 23.5 x 5.8cm*
2. *Tokay: 0.50 litre, 25.3 x 7cm*
3. *Imperial Pint: 0.60 litre, 30 x 8cm*
4. *Clavelin (Jura): 0.65 litre, 24 x 9.5cm*
5. *Rhine/Mosel: 0.70 litre, 31 x 7.5cm*
6. *Bocksbeutel (Franconia): 0.70 litre, 21.5 x 15cm*
7. *Flûte (Alsace): 0.72 litre, 33 x 7.5cm*
8. *Bordeaux: 0.75 litre, 30.5 x 7.5cm*
9. *Cream Sherry: 0.75 litre, 28x 8cm*
10. *Fino Sherry: 0.75 litre, 31 x 7.3cm*
11. *Vintage Port: 0.75 litre, 30 x 8.1cm*
12. *Bourguignonne: 0.80 litre, 30.5 x 8.2cm*
13. *Champagne: 0.80 litre, 32 x 9.5cm*
14. *Mezzo-Fiasco (Italy): 0.91 litre, 28 x 12cm*
15. *Litre: 31 x 8.5cm*

friends meet to discuss wine, on the other hand, they are vital. Eight glasses are only meagrely filled from one bottle. The answer is a magnum, which holds enough for eight to taste twice, or up to 14 to have a single proper glassful. Even larger bottles provide the same service for even larger numbers of people. Larger bottles also mature wine more slowly.

Half-bottles of fine wine are increasingly rare, except for Champagne and Sauternes, for which they are especially convenient – although recent experience with Champagne has taught me to avoid this size. (Absurdly, the pint Champagne bottle – approximately half a litre and accepted as fine for medium-term storage – is now illegal.) For red wines it is found

that the extra expense of two bottles, corks, capsules and labels is scarcely justified, when the matured wine is likely to be less good. In theory the slightly faster maturing speed of a half-bottle should allow one, effectively, to peer into the future of a long-ageing wine. In practice the wine in half-bottle is unlikely to give either an accurate or encouraging picture of the larger bottles.

Bottle sizes larger than a magnum have the practical purpose already mentioned. They also have obvious ceremonial connotations. They are, however, difficult to handle, needing two people to decant them steadily – not to mention a large number of decanters. Moreover the risk of one bad cork tainting so much wine is awful to contemplate.

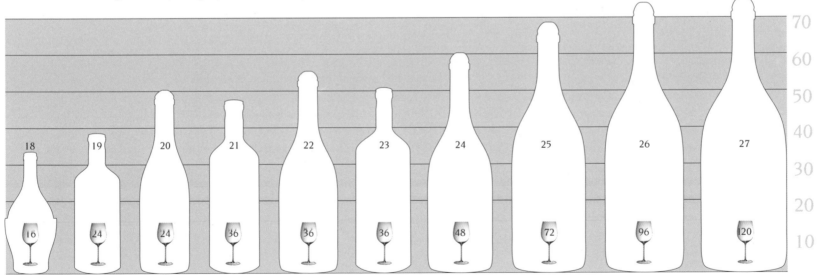

Height in cms

16. *Magnum (Bordeaux): 1.50 litres, 35.5 x 10cm*
17. *Magnum (Champagne): 1.60 litres, 39.1 x 11cm*
18. *Fiasco (Italy): 2.00 litres, 34 x 14cm*

19. *Double Magnum (Bordeaux): 3.00 litres, 39 x 13cm*
20. *Jereboam (Champagne): 3.20 litres, 49.8 x 13.5cm*
21. *Jereboam (Bordeaux): 4.50 litres, 47.2 x 14cm*

22. *Rehoboam (Champagne): 4.80 litres, 55.9 x 15.8cm*
23. *Impériale (Bordeaux): 6.00 litres, 50.8 x 15.2cm*
24. *Methuselah (Champagne): 6.40 litres, 61 x 17cm*

25. *Salmanazer (Champagne): 9.60 litres, 66 x 20.1cm*
26. *Balthazar (Champagne): 12.80 litres, 72 x 21.1cm*
27. *Nebuchadnezzer (Champagne): 16.00 litres, 97 x 22.3cm*

Temperature

It is hard to exaggerate the importance of temperature to the full enjoyment of wine, but equally hard to lay down simple guidelines for getting it right.

The ideal storage temperature of 50°F (10°C) also greatly simplifies the serving of all wines except fine reds. White wines; Champagne; rosés; Beaujolais and other light reds can all, if necessary, be taken directly from the rack and opened without further preparation. Opinions vary about the ideal temperature for different white wines, particularly sparkling and sweet ones. The standard French recommendation for Champagne is 45°F (7°C); for Sauternes is 46–48°F (8–9°C).

The weather or temperature of the room is a significant factor. If either is very warm the wine profits by being chilled to as low as 40°F (5°C); both because the drinkers need refreshing and because it will rapidly warm up to (and beyond) the ideal drinking temperature while it is being served, passed round and lingered over between sips.

If the wine is stored at a higher temperature, or conditions are warm, the only truly efficient way of chilling it is by immersion in icy water. A refrigerator is fine, with forethought. But what a fridge achieves in an hour an ice-bucket achieves in ten minutes or less. The ice-bucket should be about half-full of ice and water, depending on the size and number of bottles. The object is to immerse the bottle right up to the neck. A handful of salt speeds up the cooling process further. Indoors, wine served from an ice-bucket requires a napkin for drips – from both bottle and bucket (do not put a bucket straight on to unprotected furniture).

Achieving the perfect serving temperature for red wines is not so easy. Individual tastes (and national tastes) vary. The traditional notion of "room temperature" is meaningless when dining rooms may be anything from 60–75°F(16–24°C). The best rule of thumb is that all red wines should be just cool enough to refresh the palate.

The precise temperature that achieves this, and yet brings out the aromas of the wine, is somewhere between 55°F (13°C) and 64°F (18°C). The more full-bodied the wine, the higher the ideal temperature within this range. Thus a light and fragrant Volnay is delectable at 58°F (14°C), whereas a weighty Chambertin shows off its scents and substance better at about 63°F (17°C). "Everyday" Bordeaux Rouge is perfect at 55°F (13°C), but a Médoc Cru Classé should be 5–6°F warmer, or its luxurious aromas are muffled and indistinct.

There is a point, usually well above 70°F (21°C) where any wine begins to smell merely heady and alcoholic, its aroma losing all freshness and complexity. There is no recovery from this state. A too-cool wine can be gently warmed into life; a too-warm wine has been butchered.

The ideal solution is a temperature-controlled environment where bottles of red wine can be prepared for serving by being stood upright two or three days before they are opened. Such a room, or cupboard, could be thermostatically adjusted to anything from 55–65°F (13–18°C). The logical standard setting is 60°F (16°C), which would be lowered in hot weather and raised slightly in cold.

Failing such a facility, warm water is just as efficient for adjusting the temperature as cold. It is perfectly sound practice to put a decanter of red wine into a bucket of water at up to 70°F (21°C) until the wine reaches the required temperature. An alternative method is to rinse your decanter with hot water, drain and then polish it until your hands tell you it will warm the wine slightly without scalding it.

Suggested serving temperatures for a range of wines

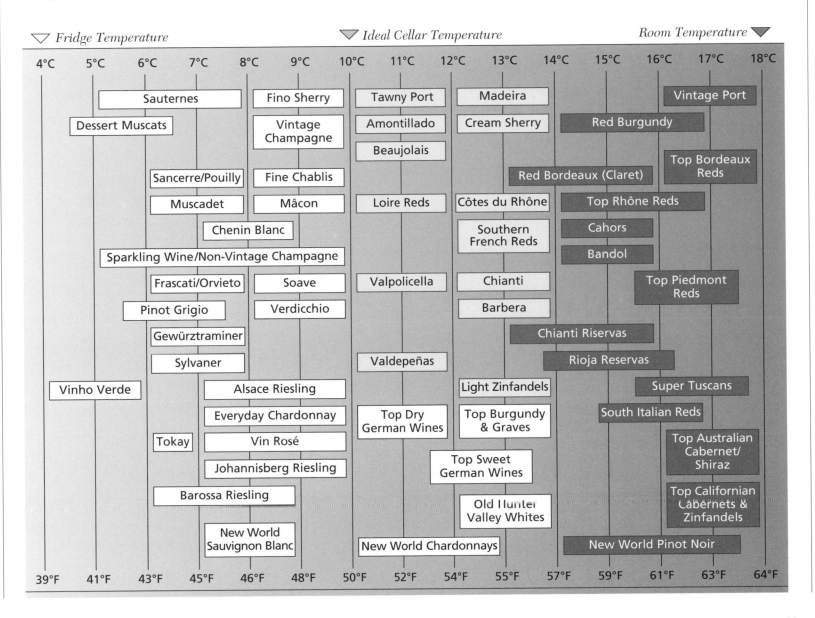

Corks, capsules & corkscrews

The history of the cork and the corkscrew makes a fascinating study. It was the cork that in the 18th century made the storage of wine to mature in bottle possible. Strange to think that before this brilliant invention nobody (except, possibly, the ancient Romans) had ever experienced the bouquet and flavour unique to old bottle-aged wine.

Once well-established in use, the cork became almost the emblem of wine itself, and the ceremony of its drawing so essential to the enjoyment of a bottle that today corks are used where a plastic bung or a screw cap would be far more appropriate, and cheaper. It is ridiculous to ram corks into the

mouths of 150 million or so bottles of Beaujolais Nouveau each year, only to tear them out again a few weeks later. A screw cap would be just as good – but what magic would be lost.

"Good wine is most frequently found among capitalists, who can afford to buy up large quantities in favourable years, the cheapest mode of purchase, who can bottle as it may be deemed most fitting for the contents of their cellars, and who have a reputation to lose."

Cyrus Redding. A History and Description of Modern Wines, 1833.

For the foreseeable future, on any wine that prides itself even remotely on its image, a cork is *de rigueur*. The routine of de-barking the cork-oaks of Portugal and Spain will go on and ingenious minds will continue to elaborate and patent new machines for taking the cork out. The latest at the time of writing is a cork with a central plunger to make a corkscrew unnecessary – but people do love corkscrews.

Fine wines intended for maturing in bottle are (or should be) plugged with extra long and fine quality corks. These call for a screw at least 5cm (2.5in.) long to grip their whole depth. Vintage port bottles are made with slightly bulbous necks to allow the cork to expand in the middle and secure an even snugger fit – which makes old port corks, thoroughly soaked in strong wine for a generation and often ready to crumble, extremely hard to extract in one piece.

The counsel of perfection with any very long-lived wine is to replace the cork at a time when it may be suspected of growing

Above: *Champagne opener in the form of a pair of pliers, "claw" for removing broken corks and waiter's friend corkscrew.*

frail. Between 20 and 25 years is the approximate age; then again, with great old treasures, at about 45 or 50 years. One Médoc first growth publicises the fact that its cellar-master will visit collectors' cellars and replace such old corks for no charge. It may be necessary to top up bottles which have distinct "ullage" (the term for airspace between wine and cork in old bottles due to slight weeping or evaporation). To do this, one bottle may have to be sacrificed to fill others. No harm is done, either, by an essential tasting to ensure that the bottle is sound.

Vintage port should also be recorked every 20 years, but in practice this is rarely done. As a result port corks often break on the corkscrew. Where this happens and crumbs of cork fall into the wine it should be filtered (a silver funnel should have a strainer fine enough to catch the crumbs). The alternative is to cut both the neck and the cork off the bottle in a dramatic-looking but very simple operation with red-hot tongs made for the purpose.

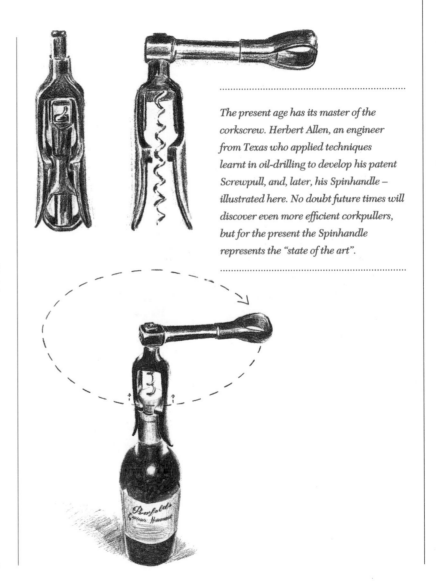

The present age has its master of the corkscrew. Herbert Allen, an engineer from Texas who applied techniques learnt in oil-drilling to develop his patent Screwpull, and, later, his Spinhandle – illustrated here. No doubt future times will discover even more efficient corkpullers, but for the present the Spinhandle represents the "state of the art".

"Wine, while yet in the Must, is usually put into open vessels; the abundance of the Spirits, i.e. the more subtle and active parts therein contained, being then so great, as not to endure imprisonment in close ones ... all parts or Elements of it being violently commoved and agitated, so that the whole mass of liquid seems to boyl, like water in a cauldron over the fire ... until all being disposed into their proper regions, the liquor becomes more pure in substance, more transparent to the eye, more piquant and gustful to the Palate, more agreeable to the Stomach, more nutritive to the Body."

The Mysterie of Vintners, 1622.

Decanting

Above: *Reproduction Georgian ringed decanters, one of magnum size, an engraved decanter and a carafe.* Right: *Once a wine is decanted it becomes anonymous, except to the person decanting: a rich vein for quiz games or trickery. Decanter labels, usually made of silver but sometimes enamel, or even gold, were apparently invented in England in the 17th century, where they were called "bottle tickets". A more recent idea is a simple silver chain on which to impale the cork.*

A lmost all wines benefit from a little aeration before drinking, particularly those that have been in bottle for some years. A mature white wine can "come alive" remarkably by being poured into the glass from a little height so that it splashes and bubbles momentarily. Red wines are customarily decanted with the same object, added to the essential one of pouring them clean from their sediment. Whether wines benefit from being decanted an hour or several before being served is frequently debated. The conventional French view is that precious aromas are dissipated by early decanting; the British view that time in the decanter softens and smooths a wine. There is no surprise in this – the French by tradition will drink their wines younger, enjoying their crispness and vigour; the British have traditionally appreciated maturity, gentleness and even the beginnings of decadence.

A simple experiment demonstrates the effect of very long aeration on vigorous wine. Decant a very good vintage port approaching maturity at say, 15 years old. Taste it straight away – it will be aggressively full of flavour, gripping your taste buds and invigorating your palate. Taste it 24 hours later; its power to shock will be slightly less, but you will find more subtleties in the smell and taste. Then stopper the decanter and keep it for a week. You will return to a tamed wine – gentle, smooth and less pungent but, to some tastes, more seductive.

To a lesser extent, that is the effect of decanting on all wines in their prime or before it. Wines beginning to tire with age can support correspondingly less aeration. Certain old burgundies never smell so ethereally sweet as immediately on opening – to miss that moment by delaying drinking them would be a shame. The decanting machine was invented for them – a device that allows the bottle to be tipped so gradually and steadily that one glass after another can be poured without disturbing the sediment and without resorting to a decanter.

Red wine with a sediment can be prepared for decanting in two ways. With sufficient foresight it can be taken from its rack and stood upright for long enough for the sediment to fall from the side of the bottle to the bottom. Sediment in certain wines is so fine that this can take two or three days. Without this preparation the bottle must be moved from its rack directly into a cradle or basket that holds it tilted just enough for the cork to be drawn. A counterpressure corkscrew is essential for this; the Screwpull ideal. The wine is then lifted from (rather than in) the cradle or basket and poured into a decanter in one continuous movement. A torch or candle is needed to throw light through the bottle so that the sediment can be seen approaching the neck and pouring stopped in time. Port bottles are very dark (and often dirty) and need a correspondingly powerful light to penetrate them. Happily their sediment is relatively stable.

Under no circumstances should wine ever be served from a basket into individual glasses, in the fashion of certain restaurants. Each tilt of the bottle will stir the sediment into the wine. Cradles and baskets only have one function – to aid in decanting. If wine is poured directly from bottle to decanter, the decanter must be tipped to meet the bottle. The alternative is to use a funnel to direct the flow. The classic form of funnel is made of silver; including a silver filter fine enough to catch fragments of cork, fitted in the top. The lower end of the spout turns sideways and directs the flow of wine against the wall of the decanter, this is to avoid the splashing of a direct fall. Straight glass funnels are also used.

Finer forms of filtration should only be used if the sediment has not settled in the bottle. Muslin is the traditional and best material. Most silver funnels will allow a layer of muslin between their inner and outer parts. As a last resort coffee filter paper can be used with a glass (or plastic) funnel. The taste of paper is (almost) removed by pouring boiling water through it first.

Above: The decanting machine keeps the bottle horizontal and allows the wine to be carefully poured into a decanter or glasses without disturbing the sediment. It is especially useful for wines with fine sediment, such as old burgundy.

"The English take great pleasure in having a quantity of excellent victuals and also in remaining a long time at table, being very sparing of wine when they drink it at their own expense."

Andrea Trevisano, Venetian Ambassador to
the court of King Henry VIII, 1497.

Cellar notes

For wines bought by the half dozen, dozen or in larger lots

Wine details

Serving record

Name

Vintage

Grower/Bottler/Shipper

Where acquired

Quantity

Bottle size

Price

Date ordered

Date received

Location in cellar

Repeat orders

Critics' comments

Date	Occasion	Bottles used	Bottles remaining

Country/Region:

Food/Other Wines	Comments	Tally

Wine details

Serving record

Name

Vintage

Grower/Bottler/Shipper

Where acquired

Quantity

Bottle size

Price

Date ordered

Date received

Location in cellar

Repeat orders

Critics' comments

Date	Occasion	Bottles used	Bottles remaining

Country/Region:

Food/Other Wines	Comments	Tally

Wine details

Serving record

Name

Vintage

Grower/Bottler/Shipper

Where acquired

Quantity

Bottle size

Price

Date ordered

Date received

Location in cellar

Repeat orders

Critics' comments

Date	Occasion	Bottles used	Bottles remaining

Country/Region:		

Food/Other Wines	Comments	Tally

Wine details

Name
....

Vintage
....

Grower/Bottler/Shipper
....

Where acquired
....

Quantity
....

Bottle size
....

Price
....

Date ordered
....

Date received
....

Location in cellar

Repeat orders
....

Critics' comments
....
....
....

Serving record

Date	Occasion	Bottles used	Bottles remaining

Food/Other Wines	Comments	Tally

Wine details

Name
....

Vintage
....

Grower/Bottler/Shipper
....

Where acquired
....

Quantity
....

Bottle size
....

Price
....

Date ordered
....

Date received
....

Location in cellar

Repeat orders
....

Critics' comments
....
....
....

Serving record

Date	Occasion	Bottles used	Bottles remaining

Country/Region:

Food/Other Wines	Comments	Tally

Wine details

Serving record

Name
....

Vintage
....

Grower/Bottler/Shipper
....

Where acquired
....

Quantity
....

Bottle size
....

Price
....

Date ordered
....

Date received
....

Location in cellar

Repeat orders
....

Critics' comments
....
....
....

Date	Occasion	Bottles used	Bottles remaining

Country/Region:

Food/Other Wines	Comments	Tally

Wine details

Serving record

Name
....

Vintage
....

Grower/Bottler/Shipper
....

Where acquired
....

Quantity
....

Bottle size
....

Price
....

Date ordered
....

Date received
....

Location in cellar

Repeat orders
....

Critics' comments
....
....
....

Date	Occasion	Bottles used	Bottles remaining

Country/Region:

Food/Other Wines	Comments	Tally

Wine details

Serving record

Name
....

Vintage
....

Grower/Bottler/Shipper
....

Where acquired
....

Quantity
....

Bottle size
....

Price
....

Date ordered
....

Date received
....

Location in cellar

Repeat orders
....

Critics' comments
....
....
....

Date	Occasion	Bottles used	Bottles remaining

Food/Other Wines	Comments	Tally

Wine details

Serving record

Name

Vintage

Grower/Bottler/Shipper

Where acquired

Quantity

Bottle size

Price

Date ordered

Date received

Location in cellar

Repeat orders

Critics' comments

Date	Occasion	Bottles used	Bottles remaining

Country/Region:

Food/Other Wines	Comments	Tally

Wine details

Name
....

Vintage
....

Grower/Bottler/Shipper
....

Where acquired
....

Quantity
....

Bottle size
....

Price
....

Date ordered
....

Date received
....

Location in cellar

Repeat orders
....

Critics' comments
....
....
....

Serving record

Date	Occasion	Bottles used	Bottles remaining

Country/Region:

Food/Other Wines	Comments	Tally

Wine details

Serving record

Name
....

Vintage
....

Grower/Bottler/Shipper
....

Where acquired
....

Quantity
....

Bottle size
....

Price
....

Date ordered
....

Date received
....

Location in cellar

Repeat orders
....

Critics' comments
....
....
....

Date	Occasion	Bottles used	Bottles remaining

Country/Region:

Food/Other Wines	Comments	Tally

Wine details

Name

Vintage

Grower/Bottler/Shipper

Where acquired

Quantity

Bottle size

Price

Date ordered

Date received

Location in cellar

Repeat orders

Critics' comments

Serving record

Date	Occasion	Bottles used	Bottles remaining

Country/Region:

Food/Other Wines	Comments	Tally

Wine details

Name
....

Vintage
....

Grower/Bottler/Shipper
....

Where acquired
....

Quantity
....

Bottle size
....

Price
....

Date ordered
....

Date received
....

Location in cellar

Repeat orders

Critics' comments
....
....
....

Serving record

Date	Occasion	Bottles used	Bottles remaining

Food/Other Wines	Comments	Tally

Wine details

Serving record

Name
....

Vintage
....

Grower/Bottler/Shipper
....

Where acquired
....

Quantity
....

Bottle size
....

Price
....

Date ordered
....

Date received
....

Location in cellar

Repeat orders
....

Critics' comments
....
....
....

Date	Occasion	Bottles used	Bottles remaining

Country/Region:

Food/Other Wines	Comments	Tally

Wine details

Name
....

Vintage
....

Grower/Bottler/Shipper
....

Where acquired
....

Quantity
....

Bottle size
....

Price
....

Date ordered
....

Date received
....

Location in cellar

Repeat orders
....

Critics' comments
....
....
....

Serving record

Date	Occasion	Bottles used	Bottles remaining

Country/Region:

Food/Other Wines	Comments	Tally

Wine details

Serving record

Name
....

Vintage
....

Grower/Bottler/Shipper
....

Where acquired
....

Quantity
....

Bottle size
....

Price
....

Date ordered
....

Date received
....

Location in cellar

Repeat orders

Critics' comments
....
....
....

Date	Occasion	Bottles used	Bottles remaining

Food/Other Wines	Comments	Tally

Wine details

Serving record

Name

Vintage

Grower/Bottler/Shipper

Where acquired

Quantity

Bottle size

Price

Date ordered

Date received

Location in cellar

Repeat orders

Critics' comments

Date	Occasion	Bottles used	Bottles remaining

	Country/Region:

Food/Other Wines	Comments	Tally

Wine details

Name

....

Vintage

....

Grower/Bottler/Shipper

....

Where acquired

....

Quantity

....

Bottle size

....

Price

....

Date ordered

....

Date received

....

Location in cellar

Repeat orders

Critics' comments

....

....

....

Serving record

Date	Occasion	Bottles used	Bottles remaining

Food/Other Wines	Comments	Tally

Wine details

Serving record

Name
....

Vintage
....

Grower/Bottler/Shipper
....

Where acquired
....

Quantity
....

Bottle size
....

Price
....

Date ordered
....

Date received
....

Location in cellar

Repeat orders

Critics' comments
....
....
....
....

Date	Occasion	Bottles used	Bottles remaining

Food/Other Wines	Comments	Tally

Wine details

Name
....

Vintage
....

Grower/Bottler/Shipper
....

Where acquired
....

Quantity
....

Bottle size
....

Price
....

Date ordered
....

Date received
....

Location in cellar

Repeat orders
....

Critics' comments
....
....
....
....

Serving record

Date	Occasion	Bottles used	Bottles remaining

Country/Region:

Food/Other Wines	Comments	Tally

Wine details

Name
....

Vintage
....

Grower/Bottler/Shipper
....

Where acquired
....

Quantity
....

Bottle size
....

Price
....

Date ordered
....

Date received
....

Location in cellar

Repeat orders
Critics' comments
....
....
....
....

Serving record

Date	Occasion	Bottles used	Bottles remaining

Country/Region:

Food/Other Wines	Comments	Tally

Wine details

Name
....

Vintage
....

Grower/Bottler/Shipper
....

Where acquired
....

Quantity
....

Bottle size
....

Price
....

Date ordered
....

Date received
....

Location in cellar

Repeat orders
....

Critics' comments
....
....
....

Serving record

Date	Occasion	Bottles used	Bottles remaining

Country/Region:

Food/Other Wines	Comments	Tally

Wine details

Serving record

Name

Vintage

Grower/Bottler/Shipper

Where acquired

Quantity

Bottle size

Price

Date ordered

Date received

Location in cellar

Repeat orders

Critics' comments

Date	Occasion	Bottles used	Bottles remaining

Country/Region:

Food/Other Wines	Comments	Tally

Wine details

Name

Vintage

Grower/Bottler/Shipper

Where acquired

Quantity

Bottle size

Price

Date ordered

Date received

Location in cellar

Repeat orders

Critics' comments

Serving record

Date	Occasion	Bottles used	Bottles remaining

Country/Region:

Food/Other Wines	Comments	Tally

Wine details

Serving record

Name
....

Vintage
....

Grower/Bottler/Shipper
....

Where Acquired
....

Quantity
....

Bottle size
....

Price
....

Date ordered
....

Date received
....

Location in cellar

Repeat orders
....

Critics' comments
....
....
....

Date	Occasion	Bottles used	Bottles remaining

Country/Region:		

Food/Other Wines	Comments	Tally

Wine details

Name

Vintage

Grower/Bottler/Shipper

Where Acquired

Quantity

Bottle size

Price

Date ordered

Date received

Location in cellar

Repeat orders

Critics' comments

Serving record

Date	Occasion	Bottles used	Bottles remaining

Food/Other Wines	Comments	Tally

Wine details

Serving record

Name

Vintage

Grower/Bottler/Shipper

Where Acquired

Quantity

Bottle size

Price

Date ordered

Date received

Location in cellar

Repeat orders

Critics' comments

Date	Occasion	Bottles used	Bottles remaining

Country/Region:

Food/Other Wines	Comments	Tally

Wine details

Serving record

Name
....

Vintage
....

Grower/Bottler/Shipper
....

Where Acquired
....

Quantity
....

Bottle size
....

Price
....

Date ordered
....

Date received
....

Location in cellar

Repeat orders
....
Critics' comments
....
....
....

Date	Occasion	Bottles used	Bottles remaining

Country/Region:

Food/Other Wines	Comments	Tally

Wine details

Name
....

Vintage
....

Grower/Bottler/Shipper
....

Where Acquired
....

Quantity
....

Bottle size
....

Price
....

Date ordered
....

Date received
....

Location in cellar

Repeat orders
....
Critics' comments
....
....
....

Serving record

Date	Occasion	Bottles used	Bottles remaining

Country/Region:

Food/Other Wines	Comments	Tally

Wine details

Name

Vintage

Grower/Bottler/Shipper

Where Acquired

Quantity

Bottle size

Price

Date ordered

Date received

Location in cellar

Repeat orders

Critics' comments

Serving record

Date	Occasion	Bottles used	Bottles remaining

Country/Region:

Food/Other Wines	Comments	Tally

Wine details

Name
....

Vintage
....

Grower/Bottler/Shipper
....

Where Acquired
....

Quantity
....

Bottle size
....

Price
....

Date ordered
....

Date received
....

Location in cellar

Repeat orders ....
Critics' comments

....

....

....

Serving record

Date	Occasion	Bottles used	Bottles remaining

Country/Region:

Food/Other Wines	Comments	Tally

Wine details

Name
....

Vintage
....

Grower/Bottler/Shipper
....

Where Acquired
....

Quantity
....

Bottle size
....

Price
....

Date ordered
....

Date received
....

Location in cellar

Repeat orders
....
Critics' comments
....
....
....
....

Serving record

Date	Occasion	Bottles used	Bottles remaining

Country/Region:		

Food/Other Wines	Comments	Tally

Wine details

Serving record

Name

....

Vintage

....

Grower/Bottler/Shipper

....

Where Acquired

....

Quantity

....

Bottle size

....

Price

....

Date ordered

....

Date received

....

Location in cellar

Repeat orders

Critics' comments

....

....

....

Date	Occasion	Bottles used	Bottles remaining

Country/Region:

Food/Other Wines	Comments	Tally

Wine details

Serving record

Name

Vintage

Grower/Bottler/Shipper

Where Acquired

Quantity

Bottle size

Price

Date ordered

Date received

Location in cellar

Repeat orders

Critics' comments

Date	Occasion	Bottles used	Bottles remaining

Food/Other Wines	Comments	Tally

Wine details

Name
....

....

Vintage
....

Grower/Bottler/Shipper
....

Where Acquired
....

Quantity
....

Bottle size
....

Price
....

Date ordered
....

Date received
....

Location in cellar

Repeat orders
....

Critics' comments
....

....

....

Serving record

Date	Occasion	Bottles used	Bottles remaining

Country/Region:

Food/Other Wines	Comments	Tally

Wine details

Serving record

Name
....

Vintage
....

Grower/Bottler/Shipper
....

Where Acquired
....

Quantity
....

Bottle size
....

Price
....

Date ordered
....

Date received
....

Location in cellar

Repeat orders
....
Critics' comments
....
....
....

Date	Occasion	Bottles used	Bottles remaining

Country/Region:

Food/Other Wines	Comments	Tally

Wine details

Name
....

Vintage
....

Grower/Bottler/Shipper
....

Where Acquired
....

Quantity
....

Bottle size
....

Price
....

Date ordered
....

Date received
....

Location in cellar

Repeat orders
....
Critics' comments
....
....
....
....

Serving record

Date	Occasion	Bottles used	Bottles remaining

Country/Region:

Food/Other Wines	Comments	Tally

Wine details

Name
....

Vintage
....

Grower/Bottler/Shipper
....

Where Acquired
....

Quantity
....

Bottle size
....

Price
....

Date ordered
....

Date received
....

Location in cellar

Repeat orders
....
Critics' comments
....
....
....

Serving record

Date	Occasion	Bottles used	Bottles remaining

Country/Region:

Food/Other Wines	Comments	Tally

Wine details

Name
....

Vintage
....

Grower/Bottler/Shipper
....

Where Acquired
....

Quantity
....

Bottle size
....

Price
....

Date ordered
....

Date received
....

Location in cellar

Repeat orders
....
Critics' comments
....
....
....

Serving record

Date	Occasion	Bottles used	Bottles remaining

Country/Region:		

Food/Other Wines	Comments	Tally

Wine details

Name

Vintage

Grower/Bottler/Shipper

Where Acquired

Quantity

Bottle size

Price

Date ordered

Date received

Location in cellar

Repeat orders

Critics' comments

Serving record

Date	Occasion	Bottles used	Bottles remaining

Food/Other Wines	Comments	Tally

Wine details

Name
....

Vintage
....

Grower/Bottler/Shipper
....

Where Acquired
....

Quantity
....

Bottle size
....

Price
....

Date ordered
....

Date received
....

Location in cellar

Repeat orders
Critics' comments
....
....
....

Serving record

Date	Occasion	Bottles used	Bottles remaining

Country/Region:

Food/Other Wines	Comments	Tally

Wine details

Name
....

Vintage
....

Grower/Bottler/Shipper
....

Where Acquired
....

Quantity
....

Bottle size
....

Price
....

Date ordered
....

Date received
....

Location in cellar

Repeat orders
....
Critics' comments
....
....
....

Serving record

Date	Occasion	Bottles used	Bottles remaining

Country/Region:		

Food/Other Wines	Comments	Tally

Wine details

Name

Vintage

Grower/Bottler/Shipper

Where Acquired

Quantity

Bottle size

Price

Date ordered

Date received

Location in cellar

Repeat orders

Critics' comments

Serving record

Date	Occasion	Bottles used	Bottles remaining

Country/Region:

Food/Other Wines	Comments	Tally

Wine details

Serving record

Name
....
....

Vintage
....

Grower/Bottler/Shipper
....

Where Acquired
....

Quantity
....

Bottle size
....

Price
....

Date ordered
....

Date received
....

Location in cellar

Repeat orders
....
Critics' comments
....
....
....

Date	Occasion	Bottles used	Bottles remaining

Country/Region:

Food/Other Wines	Comments	Tally

Wine details

Serving record

Name

Vintage

Grower/Bottler/Shipper

Where Acquired

Quantity

Bottle size

Price

Date ordered

Date received

Location in cellar

Repeat orders

Critics' comments

Date	Occasion	Bottles used	Bottles remaining

Country/Region:

Food/Other Wines	Comments	Tally

Wine details

Name
....

Vintage
....

Grower/Bottler/Shipper
....

Where Acquired
....

Quantity
....

Bottle size
....

Price
....

Date ordered
....

Date received
....

Location in cellar

Repeat orders
....

Critics' comments
....
....
....

Serving record

Date	Occasion	Bottles used	Bottles remaining

Country/Region:

Food/Other Wines	Comments	Tally

Wine details

Name

Vintage

Grower/Bottler/Shipper

Where Acquired

Quantity

Bottle size

Price

Date ordered

Date received

Location in cellar

Repeat orders
Critics' comments

Serving record

Date	Occasion	Bottles used	Bottles remaining

| Country/Region: |

Food/Other Wines	Comments	Tally

Wine details

Name

Vintage

Grower/Bottler/Shipper

Where Acquired

Quantity

Bottle size

Price

Date ordered

Date received

Location in cellar

Repeat orders

Critics' comments

Serving record

Date	Occasion	Bottles used	Bottles remaining

Country/Region:

Food/Other Wines	Comments	Tally

Wine details

Name

Vintage

Grower/Bottler/Shipper

Where acquired

Quantity

Bottle size

Price

Date ordered

Date received

Location in cellar

Repeat orders

Critics' comments

Serving record

Date	Occasion	Bottles used	Bottles remaining

Country/Region:

Food/Other Wines	Comments	Tally

Wine details

Name
....

Vintage
....

Grower/Bottler/Shipper
....

Where acquired
....

Quantity
....

Bottle size
....

Price
....

Date ordered
....

Date received
....

Location in cellar

Repeat orders
....
Critics' comments
....
....
....

Serving record

Date	Occasion	Bottles used	Bottles remaining

Country/Region:

Food/Other Wines	Comments	Tally

Wine details

Name

Vintage

Grower/Bottler/Shipper

Where acquired

Quantity

Bottle size

Price

Date ordered

Date received

Location in cellar

Repeat orders

Critics' comments

Serving record

Date	Occasion	Bottles used	Bottles remaining

	Country/Region:

Food/Other Wines	Comments	Tally

Wine details

Name
....

Vintage
....

Grower/Bottler/Shipper
....

Where acquired
....

Quantity
....

Bottle size
....

Price
....

Date ordered
....

Date received
....

Location in cellar

Repeat orders
....

Critics' comments
....
....
....

Serving record

Date	Occasion	Bottles used	Bottles remaining

Food/Other Wines	Comments	Tally

Wine details

Name

Vintage

Grower/Bottler/Shipper

Where acquired

Quantity

Bottle size

Price

Date ordered

Date received

Location in cellar

Repeat orders

Critics' comments

Serving record

Date	Occasion	Bottles used	Bottles remaining

Country/Region:

Food/Other Wines	Comments	Tally

Wine details

Name

Vintage

Grower/Bottler/Shipper

Where acquired

Quantity

Bottle size

Price

Date ordered

Date received

Location in cellar

Repeat orders
Critics' comments

Serving record

Date	Occasion	Bottles used	Bottles remaining

Country/Region:

Food/Other Wines	Comments	Tally

Wine details

Serving record

Name
....

Vintage
....

Grower/Bottler/Shipper
....

Where acquired
....

Quantity
....

Bottle size
....

Price
....

Date ordered
....

Date received
....

Location in cellar

Repeat orders
....

Critics' comments
....
....
....

Date	Occasion	Bottles used	Bottles remaining

Country/Region:

Food/Other Wines	Comments	Tally

Wine details

Name

Vintage

Grower/Bottler/Shipper

Where acquired

Quantity

Bottle size

Price

Date ordered

Date received

Location in cellar

Repeat orders

Critics' comments

Serving record

Date	Occasion	Bottles used	Bottles remaining

Country/Region:

Food/Other Wines	Comments	Tally

Wine details

Serving record

Name
....

....

Vintage
....

Grower/Bottler/Shipper
....

Where acquired
....

Quantity
....

Bottle size
....

Price
....

Date ordered
....

Date received
....

Location in cellar

Repeat orders
....

Critics' comments
....

....

....

Date	Occasion	Bottles used	Bottles remaining

Country/Region:

Food/Other Wines	Comments	Tally

Wine details

Name
....

Vintage
....

Grower/Bottler/Shipper
....

Where acquired
....

Quantity
....

Bottle size
....

Price
....

Date ordered
....

Date received
....

Location in cellar

Repeat orders
....

Critics' comments
....
....

Serving record

Date	Occasion	Bottles used	Bottles remaining

Country/Region:

Food/Other Wines	Comments	Tally

Wine details

Name
....

Vintage
....

Grower/Bottler/Shipper
....

Where acquired
....

Quantity
....

Bottle size
....

Price
....

Date ordered
....

Date received
....

Location in cellar

Repeat orders
....
Critics' comments
....
....
....

Serving record

Date	Occasion	Bottles used	Bottles remaining

Country/Region:

Food/Other Wines	Comments	Tally

Wine details

Name
....

Vintage
....

Grower/Bottler/Shipper
....

Where acquired
....

Quantity
....

Bottle size
....

Price
....

Date ordered
....

Date received
....

Location in cellar

Repeat orders
....
Critics' comments
....
....
....

Serving record

Date	Occasion	Bottles used	Bottles remaining

Country/Region:

Food/Other Wines	Comments	Tally

Wine details

Serving record

Name
....

Vintage
....

Grower/Bottler/Shipper
....

Where acquired
....

Quantity
....

Bottle size
....

Price
....

Date ordered
....

Date received
....

Location in cellar

Repeat orders
....
Critics' comments
....
....
....

Date	Occasion	Bottles used	Bottles remaining

Food/Other Wines	Comments	Tally

Wine details

Name
....

Vintage
....

Grower/Bottler/Shipper
....

Where acquired
....

Quantity
....

Bottle size
....

Price
....

Date ordered
....

Date received
....

Location in cellar

Repeat orders

Critics' comments
....
....
....

Serving record

Date	Occasion	Bottles used	Bottles remaining

Country/Region:

Food/Other Wines	Comments	Tally

Wine details

Name
....

Vintage
....

Grower/Bottler/Shipper
....

Where acquired
....

Quantity
....

Bottle size
....

Price
....

Date ordered
....

Date received
....

Location in cellar

Repeat orders
....

Critics' comments
....
....
....
....

Serving record

Date	Occasion	Bottles used	Bottles remaining

Food/Other Wines	Comments	Tally

Wine details

Name
....

Vintage
....

Grower/Bottler/Shipper
....

Where acquired
....

Quantity
....

Bottle size
....

Price
....

Date ordered
....

Date received
....

Location in cellar

Repeat orders
....
Critics' comments
....
....
....

Serving record

Date	Occasion	Bottles used	Bottles remaining

Country/Region:

Food/Other Wines	Comments	Tally

Wine details

Name
....

Vintage
....

Grower/Bottler/Shipper
....

Where acquired
....

Quantity
....

Bottle size
....

Price
....

Date ordered
....

Date received
....

Location in cellar

Repeat orders
....
Critics' comments
....
....
....

Serving record

Date	Occasion	Bottles used	Bottles remaining

Food/Other Wines	Comments	Tally

"Grudge myself good wine? As soon grudge my horse corn"

William M. Thackeray

Cellar notes

For single bottles or small quantities of wine

Received

Wine, Vintage, Source	Location	Price	Date

Opened

Date	Comments

Received

Wine, Vintage, Source	Location	Price	Date

Opened

Date	Comments

Received

Wine, Vintage, Source	Location	Price	Date

Opened

Date	Comments

Received

Opened

Wine, Vintage, Source	Location	Price	Date

Date	Comments

Received

Wine, Vintage, Source	Location	Price	Date

Opened

Date	Comments

Received

Opened

Wine, Vintage, Source	Location	Price	Date

Date	Comments

Received

Wine, Vintage, Source	Location	Price	Date

Opened

Date	Comments

Received

Wine, Vintage, Source	Location	Price	Date

Opened

Date	Comments

Received

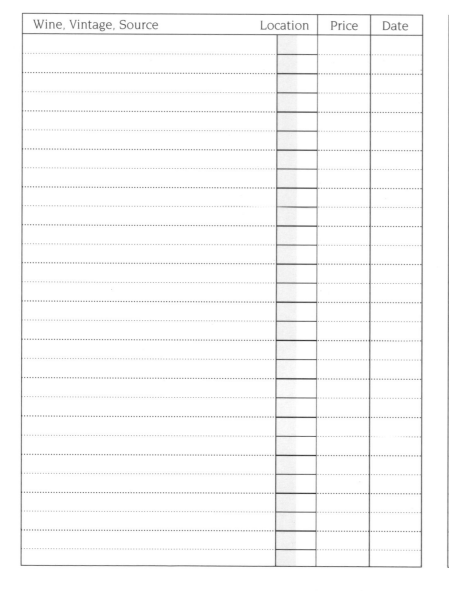

Wine, Vintage, Source	Location	Price	Date

Opened

Date	Comments

Received

Opened

Wine, Vintage, Source	Location	Price	Date

Date	Comments

Received

Opened

Wine, Vintage, Source	Location	Price	Date

Date	Comments

Received

Wine, Vintage, Source	Location	Price	Date

Opened

Date	Comments

Received

Wine, Vintage, Source	Location	Price	Date

Opened

Date	Comments

Received

Wine, Vintage, Source	Location	Price	Date

Opened

Date	Comments

Received

Wine, Vintage, Source	Location	Price	Date

Opened

Date	Comments

Received

Wine, Vintage, Source	Location	Price	Date

Opened

Date	Comments

Received

Opened

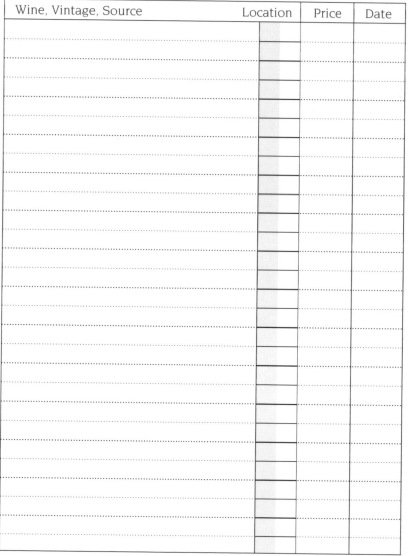

Wine, Vintage, Source	Location	Price	Date

Date	Comments

Received

Wine, Vintage, Source	Location	Price	Date

Opened

Date	Comments

Received

Opened

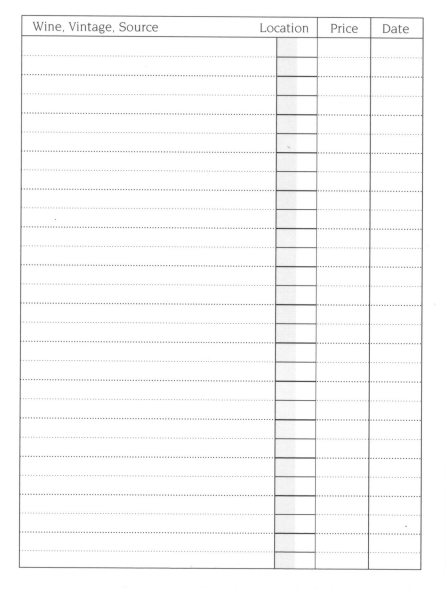

Wine, Vintage, Source	Location	Price	Date

Date	Comments

Received

Wine, Vintage, Source	Location	Price	Date

Opened

Date	Comments

Received

Wine, Vintage, Source	Location	Price	Date

Opened

Date	Comments

Received

Wine, Vintage, Source	Location	Price	Date

Opened

Date	Comments

Received

Wine, Vintage, Source	Location	Price	Date

Opened

Date	Comments

Received

Wine, Vintage, Source	Location	Price	Date

Opened

Date	Comments

Received

Wine, Vintage, Source	Location	Price	Date

Opened

Date	Comments

Received

Wine, Vintage, Source	Location	Price	Date

Opened

Date	Comments

Received

Wine, Vintage, Source	Location	Price	Date

Opened

Date	Comments

Received

Wine, Vintage, Source	Location	Price	Date

Opened

Date	Comments

Received

Wine, Vintage, Source	Location	Price	Date

Opened

Date	Comments

Memorable meals

A record of indulgence

Occasions

Date	Wine
Company	
Food	

Date	Wine
Company	
Food	

Date	Wine
Company	
Food	

Date	Wine
Company	
Food	

Date	Wine
Company	
Food	

Date	Wine
Company	
Food	

Occasions

Date	Wine
Company	
Food	

Date	Wine
Company	
Food	

Date	Wine
Company	
Food	

Date	Wine
Company	
Food	

Date	Wine
Company	
Food	

Date	Wine
Company	
Food	

Occasions

Date	Wine
Company	
Food	

Date	Wine
Company	
Food	

Date	Wine
Company	
Food	

Date	Wine
Company	
Food	

Date	Wine
Company	
Food	

Date	Wine
Company	
Food	

Occasions

Date	Wine
Company	
Food	

Date	Wine
Company	
Food	

Date	Wine
Company	
Food	

Date	Wine
Company	
Food	

Date	Wine
Company	
Food	

Date	Wine
Company	
Food	

Occasions

Date	Wine
Company	
Food	

Date	Wine
Company	
Food	

Date	Wine
Company	
Food	

Date	Wine
Company	
Food	

Date	Wine
Company	
Food	

Date	Wine
Company	
Food	

Occasions

Date	Wine
Company	

| Food | |

Date	Wine
Company	

| Food | |

Date	Wine
Company	

| Food | |

Date	Wine
Company	
Food	

Date	Wine
Company	
Food	

Date	Wine
Company	
Food	

Occasions

Date	Wine
Company	
Food	

Date	Wine
Company	
Food	

Date	Wine
Company	
Food	

Personal index

To list your wines for quick reference.

Wine	Page	Wine	Page	Wine	Page

Personal index

Wine	Page	Wine	Page	Wine	Page

Wine	Page	Wine	Page	Wine	Page